Content

Reason #1: It Oozes! — 6
Experiment #1: The Power of Spit — 8
Reason #2: It's Dirty! — 10
Experiment #2: Body Mold — 12
Reason #3: It Stinks! — 14
Experiment #3: Sour Milk — 16
Experiment #4: Gas Attack — 18
Reason #4: It Sounds Wet! — 20
Experiment #5: What Goes Down Must Come Up — 22
Reason #5: It Wiggles! — 24
Experiment #6: Dirty Drinks — 26
Reason #6: It's Weird! — 28
Experiment #7: Rubber Bone — 30

WARNING!
1. Adult supervision required for these experiments.
2. Do not eat or drink any of the experiments or ingredients.
3. Keep your experiment area clean at all times.
4. Wash your hands after each experiment.
5. Do not get any parts of the experiment near your eyes or face.

In This Kit
This kit comes with a bunch of cool stuff for hands-on fun. Check out what you get:

- **Super ooze putty**
- **Growing goo powder**
- **Liquid dropper**
- **Petri dish**

Use these components for gross activities and experiments throughout the book. Read the instructions to learn how!

So why do we get grossed out, anyway? Well, it turns out there's a **DARN GOOD REASON** for it. Through lots of hard work and experimentation, scientists have figured out that disgust is nature's way of screaming **"HANDS OFF!"** Yep, that's right. Good ol' Mother Nature gives you that overwhelming urge to **FLEE** from things that might make you sick or hurt you.

Let's look at some examples, shall we? Here are a few things that are considered gross by people EVERYWHERE.

WHY SO

BODILY FLUIDS. Spit, snot, poop, pee, barf, blood, pus, and other types of body goo *(human or animal)* carry germs. They can make you sick. Your gut reaction is to gag! The reaction is especially strong, of course, if the stuff comes from someone **ELSE'S** body. We can cope (mostly) with our own yuckiness.

BODY PARTS. Cut-off chunks of flesh **(EWWW)**, dropped scabs, hair balls, dead bodies. Like bodily fluids, they carry germs—and that gives us the ickies.

SLIMY STINKY DISGUSTING SCIENCE

Written by Kris Hirschmann
Designed by Daniel Jankowski
Cover design by Bill Henderson

All rights reserved. No part of this publication may be reproduced, or stored in a retrieval system, or transmitted in any form or by any means, electronic, mechanical, photocopying, recording, or otherwise, without written permission of Tangerine Press.

Copyright © 2012 Scholastic Inc.

an imprint of
SCHOLASTIC
www.scholastic.com

Scholastic and Tangerine Press and associated logos are trademarks and/or registered trademarks of Scholastic Inc.

Published by Tangerine Press, an imprint of Scholastic Inc., 557 Broadway; New York, NY 10012

10 9 8 7 6 5 4 3 2 1

ISBN: 978-0-545-51540-5
Printed in New Taipei City, Taiwan

THAT'S DISGUSTING!

Do you feel queasy yet? **YOU SHOULD**. All of the things on this list can trigger an instinct called **DISGUST**. It's that feeling that makes you squinch up your face, stick out your tongue, and yell, "BLECCH!!!"

What makes your stomach turn somersaults? **LOTS OF THINGS**, probably. In fact, here's a quick test. Imagine each of these things. **SEE**, **FEEL**, and **SMELL** them in your mind.

WRIGGLING MAGGOTS!
OOZING PUS!!
MOLDY, ROTTEN FOOD!!!
SEVERED FINGERS!!!!
A REEKING, POOP-FILLED TOILET!!!!!

Almost everyone experiences disgust from time to time. Different people, however, have totally different **GROSS-OUT** styles. Some folks are easily disgusted, while others can cope with all sorts of nastiness. One person might hate cockroaches with an irrational intensity. Another might faint at the sight of blood.

So what's **YOUR** story? Let's find out! Get ready to learn a little bit about the science of disgust through icky examples and awful activities, this book really pumps up the **YUCK** factor!

ROTTEN FOOD. Rotten food and drinks can make you violently ill. **YOUR BODY KNOWS THIS.** It shies away from anything that looks or smells foul.

CRITTERS. Flies, worms, maggots, lice, rats, and other critters give us the willies. They might **POISON** us. They might **INFEST** us. Or they might simply carry **GERMS**. Whatever—they're disgusting!

GROSS?

ILLNESS. Sick or diseased people and animals give us the creeps, and it's no wonder. They're obviously germ-ridden. Nature thinks you should stay far away from them—and your body obeys with a big **"BLEAH!"**

This is the **YUCK FACE.**
People all over the world make it.
Even babies make it.
It's the universal expression for **"EWWW!"**

People with a brain disorder called Huntington's disease can't tell if something is disgusting or not.

REASON #1: IT

Some gross stuff is obvious. Anyone can identify a bleeding sore or a barfing buddy. It's a no-brainer: You just **STAY AWAY** from that stuff.

Some substances, however, aren't quite so clear-cut. You can't say why, exactly, but they just **LOOK** kind of yucky. Are they really bad for you? **WHO KNOWS**? Just to be on the safe side, though, your body swings into that **DISGUST** reaction.

So what makes something look yucky? There are a few **CLUES** we use to make that decision, and the #1 clue is this:

DOES IT OOZE?

Yep. Oozing stuff skeeves us out— and it isn't hard to see why. Think about all the nasty body stuff that oozes: zit juice, blister water, pee, etc. Also think about rotting veggies, critter-filled pond slime, and other gooey things. **YUCK**! It's no wonder that we tendto think **OOZE = ICK.**

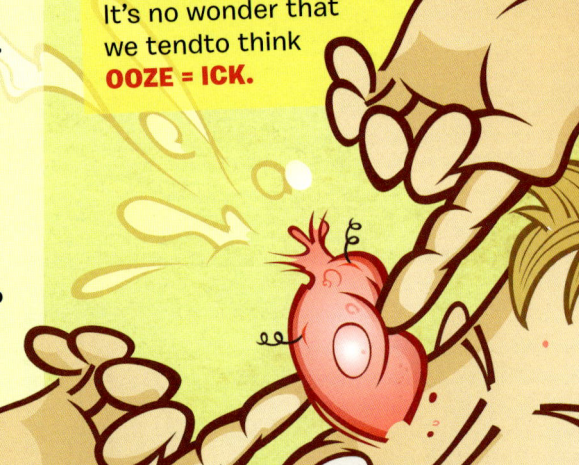

OOZES!

Activity: Slime It UP!
Guess what? **YOU'RE IN LUCK!** This kit comes with two of the coolest and **GROSSEST** slimes anywhere! One is like a putty. The other is a slippery, gooey mess. Check them out!

Wash your hands after handling any type of slime. Seriously. You don't want that stuff under your fingernails.

Super Ooze Putty

This stuff is stiff enough to squeeze, shape, and mold. As soon as you're done, though— **WHOOPSIE!** It slowly melts into a flat puddle. Watch as the putty **OOZES**, sluglike, from one shape to another. Also try shaping the putty into a bouncing ball, a long string, and anything else you can imagine. There's no end to the fun you can have with this crazy concoction!

In the science of disgust, breaking the skin is called "piercing the body envelope." People just **HATE** that. Even the thought makes us shudder!

Growing Goo Powder

This stuff is any amount of nasty you want to make it—and it's super easy! Put about ¼ teaspoon (1 ml) of the goo powder into a resealable plastic bag. Fill the liquid dropper from this kit with water and squirt it into the bag. Knead gently. The powder will turn into a revolting slime that is safe but **YUCKY** to touch!

Try adding more droppers full of water. You'll be amazed at how much liquid this **GROSS GOO** can absorb!

EXPERIMENT #1: THE POWER OF SPIT

Let's experiment with some **BODY OOZE**, shall we? You're about to observe the power of your own spit. It can actually dissolve food **OUTSIDE YOUR BODY**. Try it and see!

What You Need:
- Liquid dropper from this kit
- Small jar of sweet potato baby food *(the kind with a resealable lid)*
- Refrigerator

What You Do:

1. Open the jar of baby food. Squeeze the liquid dropper's bulb to force all the air out. Poke the dropper's tip into the baby food and release the bulb. Observe how much food, if any, gets sucked upward into the dropper.

2. Wash the dropper and set it aside.

3. Now for the gross part! Work up a great big **LOOGIE** in your mouth. Carefully hock the entire wad into the jar of baby food. **PTOOIE!**

4. Screw the lid onto the baby food. Put the jar into a refrigerator. Let it sit for one full day.

5. Label the jar **"DO NOT EAT—SCIENCE EXPERIMENT."** You don't want a family member to eat this, right?

6. Repeat step 1. Do you see a difference in the amount of food you can slurp up?

Here's the Scoop!

Spit *(or saliva, as scientists like to call it)* contains a chemical called amylase. Amylase works to break down foods that contain starch. Sweet potatoes are about as starchy as it gets, so that loogie **DIGESTS** the food right in the jar. It takes a full day for the potatoes to break down into a slippery, slimy liquid that you can suck into your dropper.

REASON #2: IT'S DIRTY!

Ooze isn't our only clue that something might be dangerous. **DIRT** and **GRIME** send up a red flag, too. Why? Well, dangerous **GERMS** lurk everywhere. We can't see them—they're way too small. But we **CAN** see grunge. We assume that if something's really dirty, it's probably germy, too.

NEED PROOF? Consider a couple of examples. Would you rather use:

A DUSTY SPOON OR A SPOTLESS ONE?

A RUST-STREAKED TOILET OR A SPARKLING ONE?

A STAINED TOWEL OR A BRAND-NEW ONE?

We could go on—but we don't need to. Science predicts **EXACTLY** which choices you'll make. Dirty stuff is **JUST GROSS**!

Dirty clumps called dust bunnies can build up under people's furniture. Dust bunnies are made of hair, lint, dead skin, spiderwebs, and other gross goodies. They provide homes for mites and other grime-loving critters.

Germs, Germs, Germs!

"Germs" isn't a specific term. It's kind of a catchall word for a bunch of yucky microorganisms *(living things that are too small to see without a microscope)*. There are four main types of germs:

- **Viruses.** These tiny infectious agents can only multiply inside a body. They cause colds, the flu, and many other diseases.

- **Bacteria.** These one-celled organisms can multiply inside or outside a body. They cause infections.

- **Protozoa**. These one-celled organisms thrive in wet places. They can cause diarrhea, nausea, and other digestive problems.

- **Fungi**. These many-celled organisms grow like plants when conditions are good. Some fungi can grow in or on human flesh.

Some people have a crippling fear of germs. This fear is called mysophobia.

EXPERIMENT #2: BODY

Do you need proof that germs are lurking everywhere? Look no further than your very own body! This experiment will show you some of the nasties that live in and on your skin.

What You Need:

- Fresh bakery-type bread *(the kind with no preservatives)*
- Several resealable plastic bags
- Liquid dropper from this kit
- Water
- Marker

MOLD

What You Do:

1. Avoid bathing or showering for at least 24 hours. If you can get away with it for longer, that's **EVEN BETTER**.

2. Run around and get a little sweaty, if possible. Then take a piece of bread. Use the liquid dropper to put a few drops of water onto the bread. Rub the damp bread under your nasty **ARMPITS**.

3. Put the bread into a resealable plastic bag. Seal the bag and use the marker to label the bag "**ARMPITS**."

4. Repeat steps 2 and 3 to create bread Baggies from your **FEET**, your **FOREHEAD**, and any other parts of your body you care to test.

5. Set the Baggies in a nice, warm place and wait a few days. Then check to see what's **GROWING** on!

HERE'S THE SCOOP!

Germs settle on your skin **ALL DAY LONG**. You're basically a walking, talking collection of bacteria, viruses, and fungi. When you scrub yourself down with bread, you remove whole colonies of the little beasties. The bacteria and fungi happily multiply in their warm, moist, bread-filled new home. That's right. That stuff in those bags? It came from **YOU**!

REASON #3: IT

Bad smells have a **HUGE** yuck factor. **THINK ABOUT IT.** You can probably come up with a whole **LIST** of odors you can't stand. In case you can't, though, here are some things for you to consider:

A BAG OF USED BABY DIAPERS

A STEAMING PILE OF DOG POOP

FRESH-FROM-THE-STOMACH VOMIT

DIRTY GYM SOCKS

ROTTEN EGGS

A FULL GARBAGE TRUCK

Are you imagining these smells? If so, you're probably making the **YUCK FACE** right now. *(See page 5 if you don't remember what the **YUCK FACE** looks like. Or just take a peek in a mirror.)*

Why do we find these smells so horrible? It's the same old story. Human and animal waste, body fluids, and decaying food might be dangerous to us. Their **AWFUL ODORS** convince you to stay far, far away!

The odor of human poop is the world's most offensive smell. Studies show that just about **EVERYONE** hates this particular stench.

EXPERIMENT #3: SOUR MILK

On any list of stinky "food gone bad," sour milk has got to earn one of the top spots. This stuff smells **FOUL**! Make some milk go bad and sniff the revolting results for yourself.

What You Need:
- Petri dish from this kit
- Liquid dropper from this kit
- Skim milk
- Vinegar
- Spoon

What You Do:

1. Fill the petri dish about halfway with skim milk.

2. Use the liquid dropper to add vinegar to the milk, drop by drop. Use the spoon to stir the mixture after each drop. Repeat until the milk gets **CLUMPY** and **YUCKY**.

3. Put your nose down close to that nasty stuff. Take a **GREAT BIG WHIFF**. How does it smell? Not too bad, right?

4. Dump the contents of the petri dish down your sink. Wash and dry the petri dish.

5. Fill the petri dish halfway with skim milk again. Leave the dish uncovered in a warm place. Check the dish once a day until the milk clumps up. Once it does, let the dish sit for another 24 hours.

6. Once again, prepare your sniffer. Get right down there and smell your work. **WHEW! THAT'S STRONG**!

Here's the Scoop!

Substances called acids make milk curdle *(clump up)*. Vinegar is an acid. When you add it to the milk, the curdling process happens quickly and cleanly. Thankfully for your nose, **IT DOESN'T STINK**.

When you let milk curdle naturally, the process is completely different. Natural curdling happens as bacteria digest milk. This process creates a substance called lactic acid. When the acid level gets high enough, the milk clumps. By this time, of course, the milk is **LOADED** with nasty bacteria. It's all those bacteria that **REEK**—not the milk itself. That horrible smell? It's nature's signal that the milk is loaded with germs. **RUN AWAY, RUN AWAY!**

EXPERIMENT #4: GAS ATTACK

You've already made milk reek. Now it's time to do the same job on yourself! Pick various foods and test them to discover their gas-producing power. Have fun rating the resulting emissions!

What You Need:
- Foods and drinks from the chart on page 19
- Pen or pencil

What You Do:
1. Choose **ONE** of the foods or drinks from the chart on page 19. Consume a nice big serving of it.
2. Wait a while. It's hard to say exactly how long, because the effect might come on **QUICKLY**, after **A FEW HOURS**, or **NOT AT ALL**. Just pay attention to your rear-end region for about 4 to 8 hours.
3. If a gas attack erupts, refer to the chart! Circle the "yes" next to the item you consumed. Rate the gas on its **AMOUNT** and **RANKNESS**. 1 is mild. 5 is severe!
4. If no gas appears, circle the "No". **OH WELL**.
5. Repeat steps 1 through 4 with other foods to complete the chart. Test only one food per day. Otherwise maybe you've **SMELT** it, but you won't know which food **DEALT** it!

Here's the Scoop!

Lots of helpful bacteria live in your large intestine. These bacteria break down certain foods. This process releases hydrogen, carbon dioxide, and sometimes methane gas. These gases and others escape from your, um, **REAR END** in the form of farts (officially known as flatus). They carry smelly compounds that give your toots that delicious, disgusting **STENCH**. The quantity and smell of the gas vary depending on the food that produced it.

Gives Me Gas??

Food	Gas?	Amount	Smell (1 to 5)
Beans (not green)	No/Yes	____	____
Red Legumes	No/Yes	____	____
Veggies:			
Broccoli	No/Yes	____	____
Brussels sprouts	No/Yes	____	____
Asparagus	No/Yes	____	____
Onions	No/Yes	____	____
Corn	No/Yes	____	____
Peas	No/Yes	____	____
Dairy:			
Milk	No/Yes	____	____
Cheese	No/Yes	____	____
Ice cream	No/es	____	____
Yogurt	No/Yes	____	____
Other:			
Artificial sweeteners	No/Yes	____	____
Fresh fruit	No/Yes	____	____
Nuts	No/Yes	____	____
Fizzy drinks	No/Yes	____	____
Other: _____	No/Yes	____	____

REASON #4: IT SO

Your stomach probably doesn't turn when you take a shower or wash the dishes. Of course! Shower and sink water is nice and clean. It can't hurt you, so it doesn't disgust you.

But what if you hear some kind of wet, oozy, **GOOPY** sound that you can't identify?

Well, that's a totally different story. Your imagination goes wild picturing the source of the sound. Is it a giant alien **SLIME BLOB**? A slithering **SNAKE**? Or maybe just a friend with a really bad **HEAD COLD**? Who knows? But whatever it is, it probably isn't good! Or that's what nature **WANTS** you to think, anyway.

It's the same old story. Wet things can be all **KINDS** of nasty. Think about these things:

Mold and mildew thrive in damp conditions. Yucky bodily fluids are wet, wet, wet! Poop isn't a fluid, but it's wet, too—ick! Oozing mud and muck provide homes for dangerous critters. Many germs need moisture to grow.

…UNDS WET!

The yuckiest places in your home are all **WET**! Studies show that the five germiest spots in people's houses are:

1. The toilet bowl
2. The kitchen drain
3. Kitchen sponges
4. The kitchen sink

Damp conditions in these places let dangerous bacteria thrive.

Can you come up with more examples? Probably. List some **WET** or **GOOEY** things and places that disgust you. Then think about how each thing might hurt you. There'll be a connection—guaranteed.

Fun Vocabulary Fact!
Words that imitate sounds are called onomatopoeia. **SPLAT, GLOP, SLURP, FLAAARP,** and **SQUISH** are a few goopy examples!

EXPERIMENT #5:

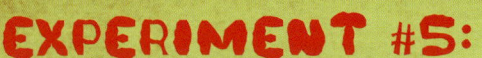

WHAT GOES DOWN MUST COME UP

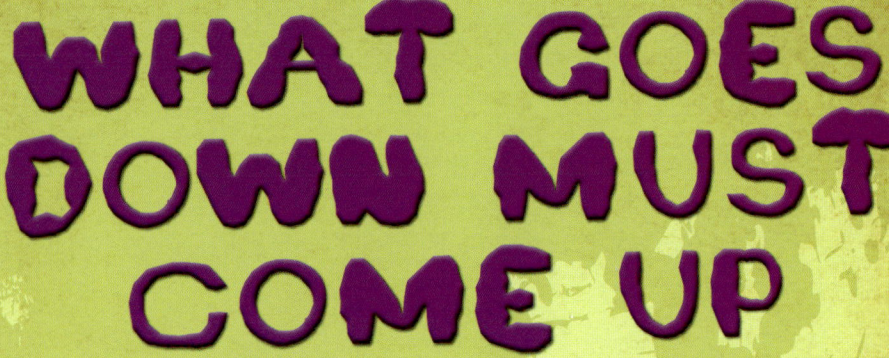

The sound of a really juicy **BELCH** definitely gives some people the **WET WILLIES.** Turbo-power your burps and enjoy your friends' revolted responses!

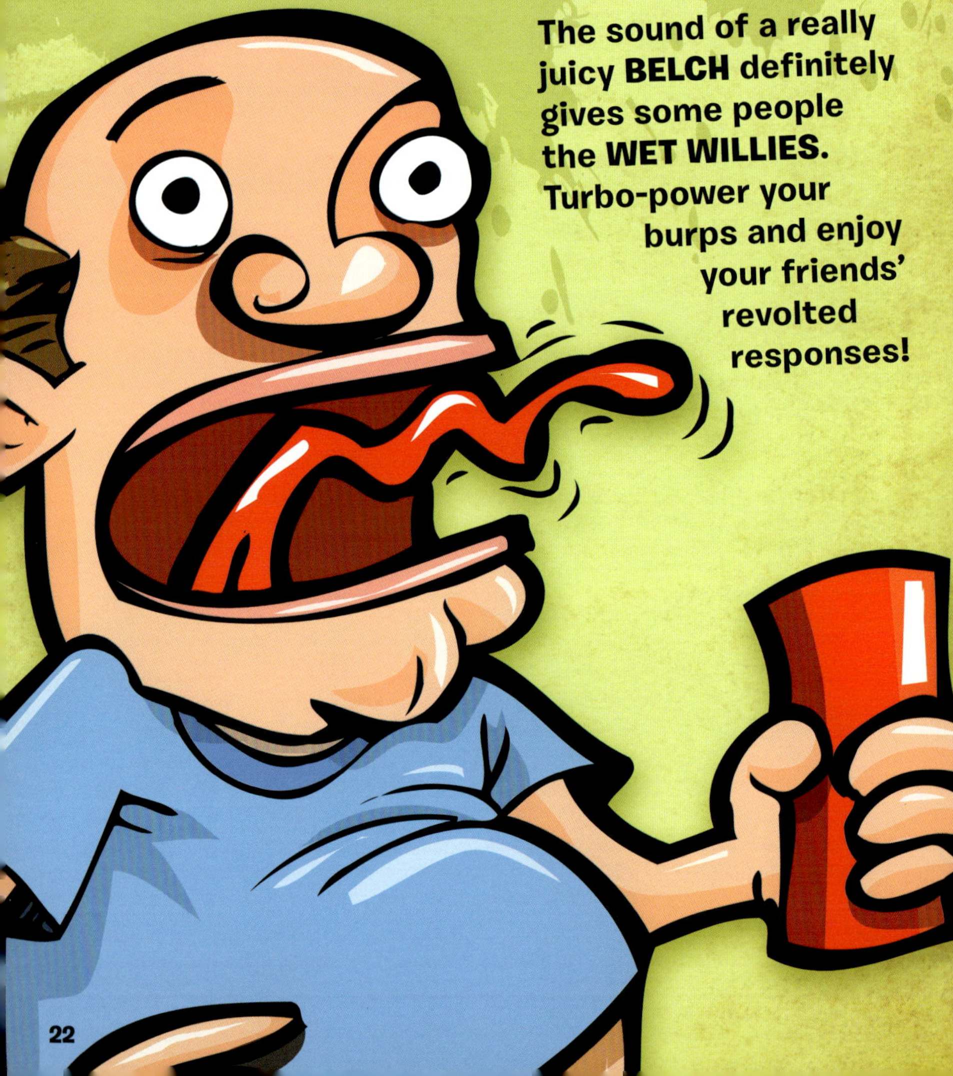

What You Need:
- One can of carbonated soda
- Drinking straw

What You Do:
1. Open a can of soda. Insert a straw.
2. Drink the entire soda through the straw as quickly as you can. Really suck it down!
3. In a minute or two, you'll feel an odd **BUBBLING** sensation in your stomach. Then you'll feel the urge to let those bubbles loose. Let the **BELCH-A-THON** begin!

Here's the Scoop!
There are a couple of things to discuss here. Let's talk about those magnificent **BELCHES** first. Soda contains a gas called carbon dioxide. When you drink the soda, you gulp down all that gas, too—and drinking through a straw pumps up the **FIZZ EFFECT**. Your belly gets gassier and gassier until ... **URRRRP**! Up it all comes!

But why does it **SOUND** so gross? Well, that's a different effect. The carbon dioxide exits your stomach with **FORCE**. It blasts its way through your throat on its way to freedom. The loose tissues of your throat vibrate wetly. That's what makes that classic **BURP** sound. The volume of the belch depends on the force of the gas!

REASON #5: IT

Imagine you're sitting at home, watching TV, when an unexpected motion catches your attention. You turn your head to look and ... **EWWW! THERE'S A GIANT COCKROACH CRAWLING UP YOUR WALL!** Let the screeching begin!!!

Or how about this one? You're walking down a city street. All of a sudden a fat RAT pops out of a sewer and skitters right across your toes. GROSS!! You just might SHUDDER with disgust!

We could go on, but really, do we need to? The basic fact is that most people think wiggly things are **YUCKY**. This is true evenif the wiggly things in question are harmless. See, nature doesn't care. **SOME** snakes can hurt you, so it's best to stay away from **ALL** of them. **SOME** rodents carry diseases and bite, so **WHY TAKE THE CHANCE**? We're programmed to find them disgusting, each and every one!

WIGGLES!

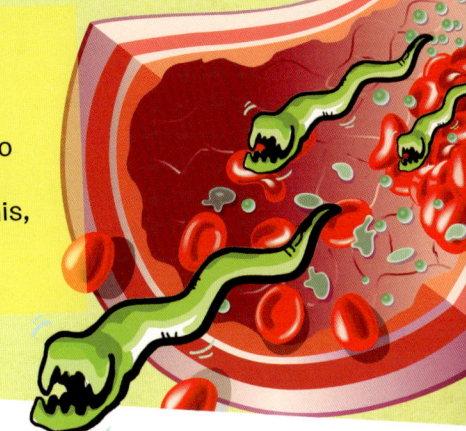

Wriggly critters called hookworms burrow right into the bottoms of people's bare feet. They use the person's blood vessels like roads to travel to the lungs, intestines, and other organs. With behavior like this, is it any **WONDER** we find wiggly things gross?

Which critters give YOU the creeps? Think about it. Why do you think you hate those things so much?

Grossest Critters (According to Me)

1. _____
2. _____
3. _____
4. _____

In a classic science experiment, a person watches while a sterile (dirt-and germ-free) bug is dipped into a delicious drink. The person then gets to choose between the delicious drink and a gross but bug-free one. The result is a big shocker—**NOT**!! Everyone chooses the disgusting drink. They don't care how clean that bug is. They don't want to touch anything **IT** has touched!

25

EXPERIMENT #6: DIRTY

Would your friends drink **ROACH JUICE**? How about **WORM WATER**? Find out with a truly **TERRIBLE** taste test!

What You Need:
- One small plastic critter. It could be a roach, a worm, a fly, or anything else you have handy. Choose the yuckiest, most realistic critter you can find.
- Two clear drinking glasses
- Grown-up helper
- Water
- Cooking pot

DRINKS

What You Do:

1. Get a **GROWN-UP HELPER** to sterilize the plastic critter for you. To do this, the critter should sit in boiling water for about five minutes. The hot water will kill any germs that might be clinging to the critter.

2. Drop the sterilized critter into a clear drinking glass. Fill the glass with water. Get another glass and fill that one with water, too.

3. Offer the drinks to an unsuspecting friend. Tell the friend to take a sip from whichever drink he or she likes. Record which glass the friend chooses: **CRITTER** or **NON-CRITTER**.

4. Repeat steps 2 and 3 with as many friends as possible. What results do you get?

Here's the Scoop!

Unless your friends just love to be gross, they'll probably show a strong preference for the **CRITTER-FREE** water. This should be true even if you tell them the critter is **FAKE** and **CLEAN**. Why? Well, critters are **WIGGLY**. Critters are **GROSS**. Your brain may know you're safe, but your body isn't taking any chances. It activates that disgust reaction … just in case!

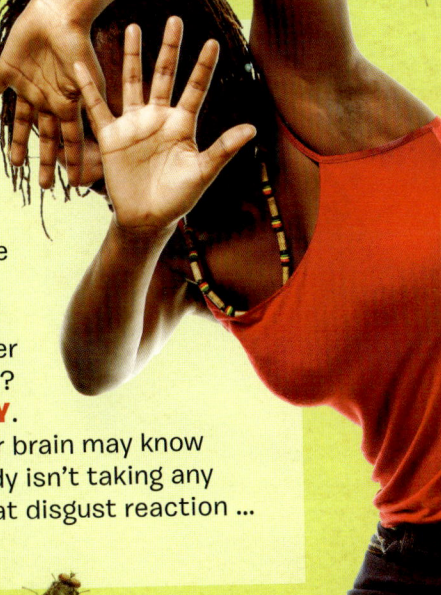

REASON #6:

If you're like most people, you have a very orderly little brain. You expect things to **LOOK** and **ACT** certain ways. If something seems **OFF**—well, alarm bells go off. Your gut **DISGUST** reaction tells you to **STAY AWAY** until you figure out whether you're safe or not.

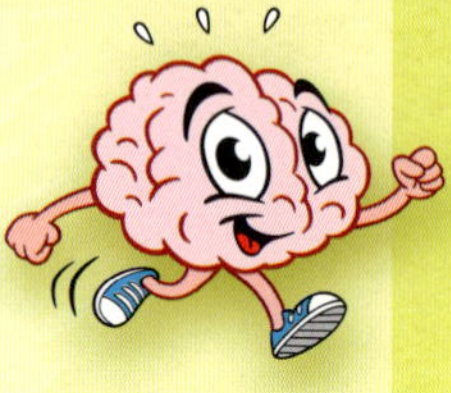

Let's say, for example, you see a person covered in **RED SLIME**. Let's also say you're pretty sure the slime is some type of gelatin dessert. You're not positive, though. You feel grossed out, and you'll keep your distance until you know **EXACTLY** what that slime is.

WEIRD!

Or what about weird **FOOD**? That's a classic! Imagine your plate is piled high with something that smells delicious, but which seems to be **MOVING** slightly. Or maybe it has creepy **TENTACLES** poking out of it. Or maybe it's an odd greenish-brownish color. For some reason, it's just **NOT RIGHT**.

There's **NO WAY** you're putting that stuff into your mouth.

Can you come up with your own examples? Think of something you love. Then imagine that it smells bad, or bends the wrong way, or is maggot-infested, or has some other bizarre defect. **YUCK**! See how easy it is to turn good into **GROSS**?

Your ideas about weird food are probably very different depending on where in the world you live. In America, for example, people don't eat a lot of bugs. The very idea is considered **GNARLY**. In other countries, though, insects are a tasty treat. No **GROSS-OUT FACTOR** there!

You can teach yourself to become less disgusted by certain things. The trick is to expose yourself to them a **LOT**. This technique is called desensitization. Therapists sometimes use it to help people overcome their fears.

EXPERIMENT #7: RUBBER

Bones are supposed to be hard. But what if they weren't? What if they were all gooey and bendy, like pieces of rubber? That would be **DISGUSTING**— as you're about to see for yourself!

What You Need:
- **Chicken leg or thigh bone**
- **White vinegar** *(lots)*
- **Jar with a screw-on lid**
  (must be big enough to hold your chicken bone)

What You Do:
1. Clean the chicken bone thoroughly. Don't leave any stray scraps of **FLESH** or **BLOOD** clinging to it. **EWWW**!
2. Put the chicken bone into the jar.
3. Pour just enough vinegar into the jar to cover the bone. Screw the lid onto the jar and put your experiment in a safe place.
4. After three days, open the jar and pour the vinegar down the sink. Gently try to bend the bone. Does anything **WEIRD** happen? Not yet, probably.

BONE

5. Repeat steps 2 through 4 a few times. One day you'll discover that the bone is flexible, rubbery … and **TOTALLY REVOLTING**!

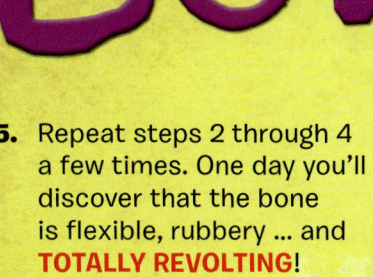

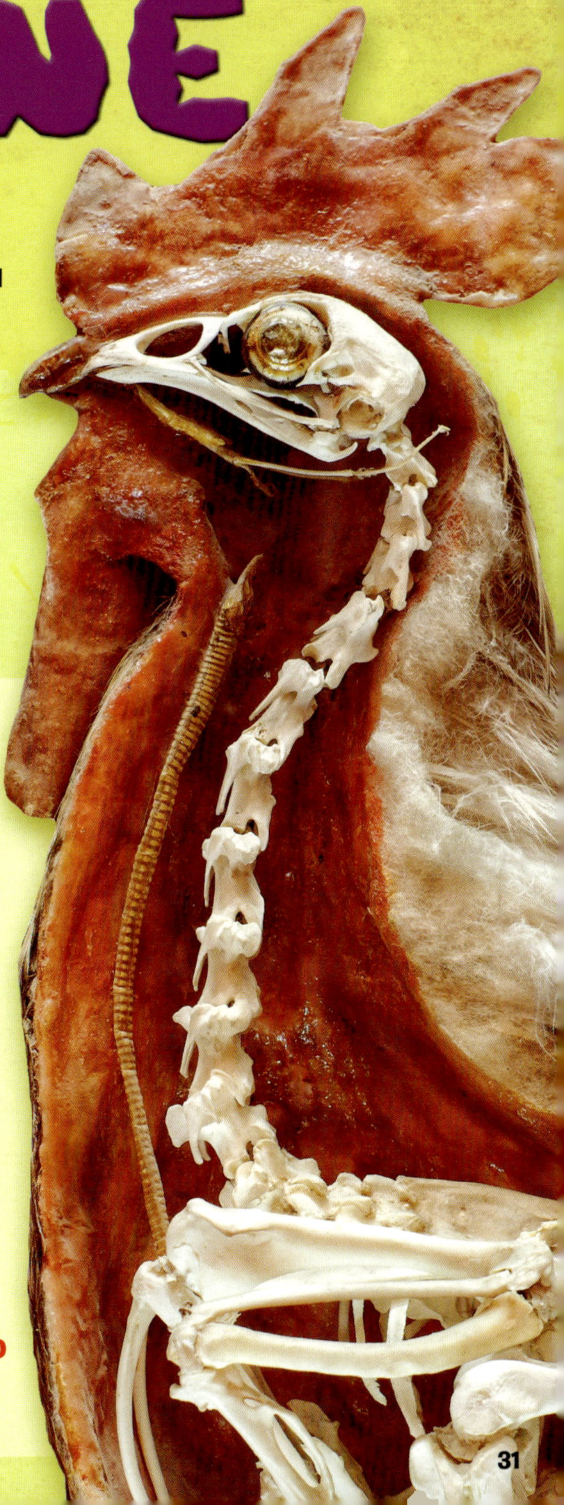

Here's the Scoop!

Bones contain many minerals, including calcium carbonate and calcium phosphate. These minerals make bones hard. When you put a bone into vinegar or any other acid, a chemical reaction takes place between the acid and the calcium compounds. The acid eats away the calcium and dissolves it into liquid. If the reaction continues long enough, all the calcium will be gone. Only cartilage and other rubbery materials remain. You've created a bendy bone that looks **RIGHT**, but acts **OH SO WRONG**. It's **GROSS** in the **COOLEST** possible way!!!

GLOSSARY

YOU LEARNED SOME GREAT WORDS IN THIS BOOK! HERE'S A LIST, WITH DEFINITIONS, TO REMIND YOU OF YOUR DISGUSTING BUT AMAZING JOURNEY.

Acid A chemical compound that tastes sour and has extra hydrogen atoms. Strong acids can break down many substances.

Amylase A digestive enzyme *(chemical)* found in human saliva.

Curdle To separate a mixture into its liquid and solid parts.

Desensitization The process of becoming less sensitive to or disgusted by something.

Disgust An emotional and physical response to things we find gross.

Flatus Gas expelled from the digestive tract through the anus.

Microorganism A living organism that is too small to see without a microscope.

Mysophobia An unusually strong or crippling fear of germs.

Onomatopoeia A word that tries to imitate a sound.

Sterile Completely free of microorganisms.

Sulfur An element that creates a strong smell when it combines with certain other elements.